ADELE
FOR UKULELE

Cover photo by Joern Pollex / Stringer

ISBN 978-1-4950-9220-6

HAL•LEONARD®
7777 W. BLUEMOUND RD. P.O. BOX 13819 MILWAUKEE, WI 53213

Visit Hal Leonard Online at
www.halleonard.com

Chasing Pavements

Words and Music by Adele Adkins and Francis Eg White

Hello

Words and Music by Adele Adkins and Greg Kurstin

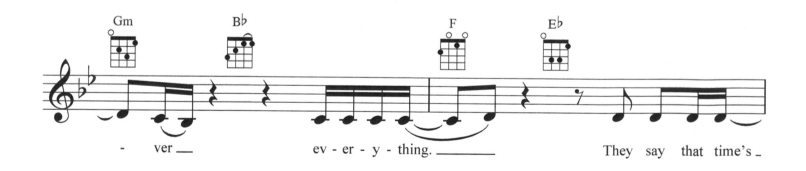

Verse

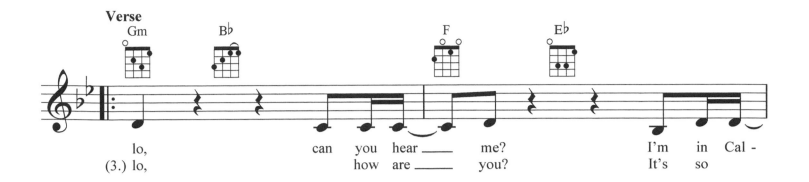

lo, can you hear ____ me? I'm in Cal -
(3.) lo, how are ____ you? It's so

- i-for - nia dream - ing a - bout who ____ we used ____ to be ____ when we were young -
typ - i-cal ____ of me ____ to talk ____ a - bout ____ my-self; ____ I'm sor - ry. I hope ____

- er ____ and free. ____ I've for - got -
that you're well. ____ Did you ev -

- ten how ____ it felt ____ be - fore ____ the world ____ fell at ____ our feet. There's such a
- er make ____ it ____ out ____ of that town where noth - ing ev - er hap - pened? It's no

Pre-Chorus

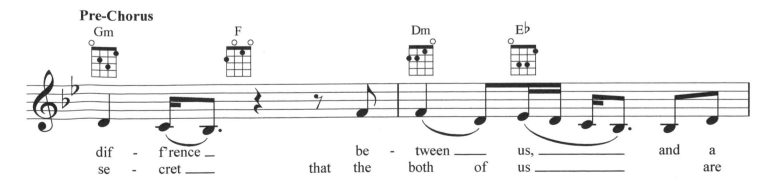

dif - f'rence ____ be - tween ____ us, ____ and a
se - cret ____ that the both of us ____ are

Lovesong

**Words and Music by Robert Smith, Laurence Tolhurst, Simon Gallup, Paul S. Thompson,
Boris Williams and Roger O'Donnell**

How - ev - er far ___ a - way, _____ I will al - ways love __ you.

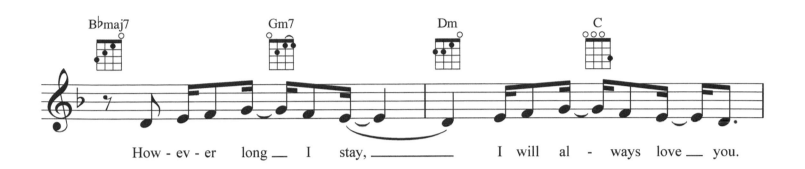

How - ev - er long ___ I stay, _____ I will al - ways love __ you.

To Coda ⊕

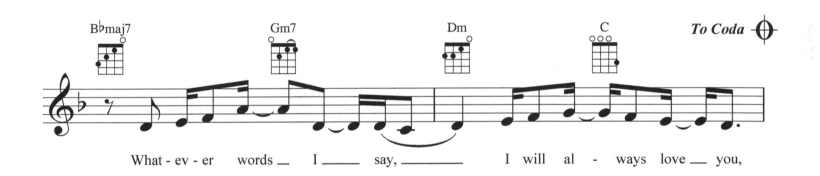

What - ev - er words ___ I ___ say, _____ I will al - ways love __ you,

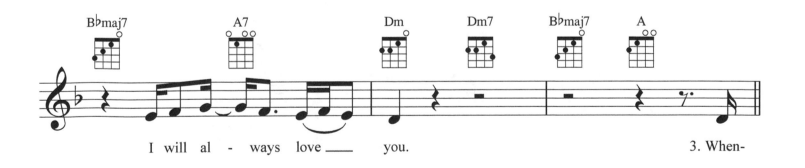

I will al - ways love ___ you.   3. When-

Verse

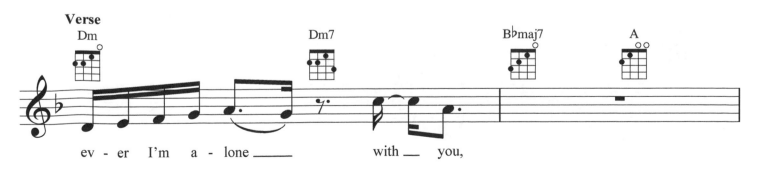

ev - er I'm a - lone _____ with __ you,

you make — me feel — like I am — free a - gain. — When -

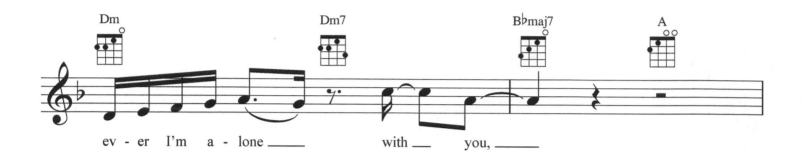

ev - er I'm a - lone ___ with ___ you, ___

D.S. al Coda

you make — me feel — like I am — clean a - gain. —

Coda

Interlude

I will al - ways love ___ you. ___

Outro-Chorus

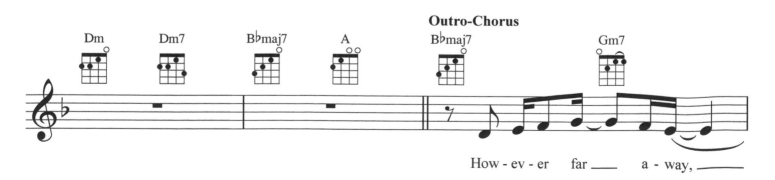

How - ev - er far ___ a - way, ___

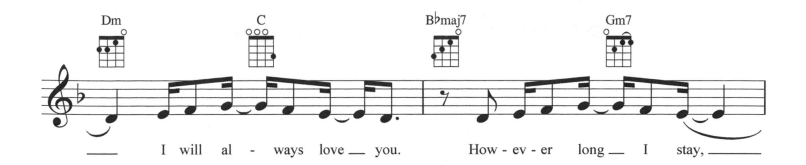

I will al - ways love ___ you. How - ev - er long ___ I stay, _____

I will al - ways love ___ you. What - ev - er words ___ I ___ say, ___

I will al - ways love you, I'll al - ways ___

___ love you. ___ I'll al - ways ___ love you. _____ 'Cause I love ___ you. ___

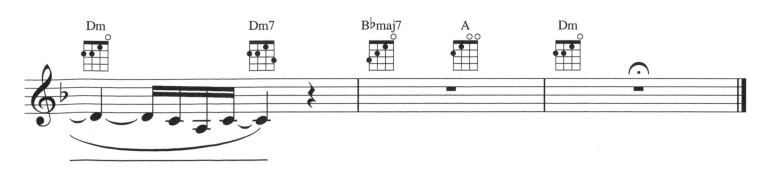

Make You Feel My Love

Words and Music by Bob Dylan

1. When the rain __ is blow-ing in your face __
2. When the eve - ning __ shad-ows and the stars ap - pear, __

and the whole __ world is on __ your case, __
and there is no __ one there to dry __ your tears, __

I could of - fer you a warm em - brace __
I could hold __ you for a mil - lion __ years __

to make you feel my love. __

Bridge

I know you have - n't made your mind up yet, __

but I would nev - er do ___ you wrong. ___

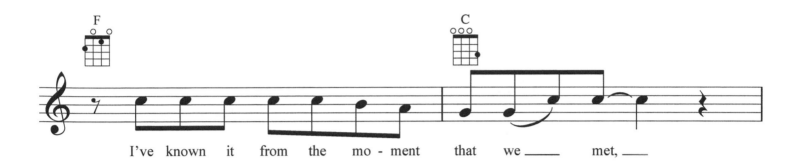

I've known it from the mo - ment that we ___ met, ___

no doubt in my mind where you be - long. ___

Verse

3. I'd go hun - gry, I'd ___ go ___ black and blue, ___

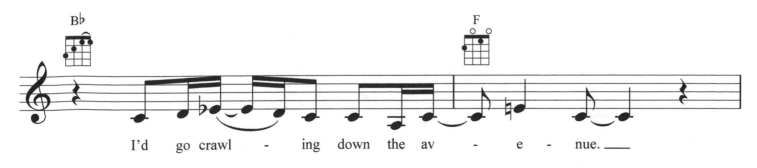

I'd go crawl - ing down the av - e - nue. ___

15

Know there's noth - ing that ___ I ___ would - n't do ___

to make you feel my love. ___

Bridge

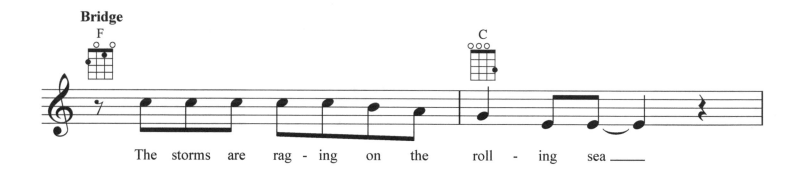

The storms are rag - ing on the roll - ing sea ___

and on the high - way of re - gret. ___

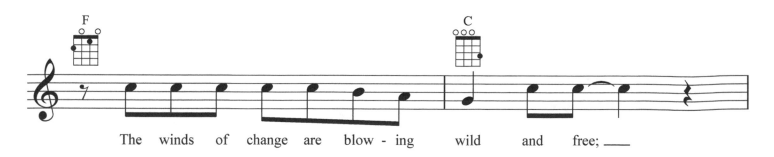

The winds of change are blow - ing wild and free; ___

you ain't seen noth - ing like me yet. _____

Outro-Verse

I can make you hap - py, make your _ dreams come true. _

Noth - ing that I _____ would - n't ____ do.

Go to the ends of the _ earth for you, _ to make you feel my love, _

_ to make you feel my love. _

17

Rumour Has It

Words and Music by Adele Adkins and Ryan Tedder

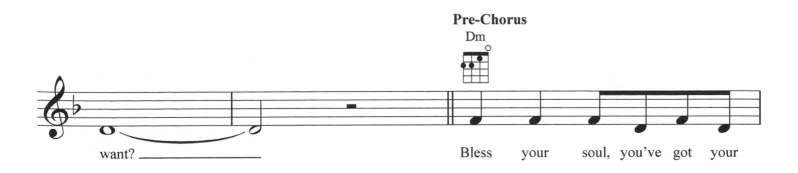

want? _____

Pre-Chorus

Bless your soul, you've got your

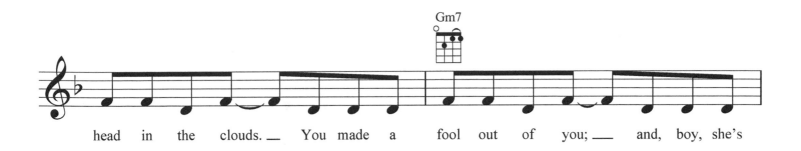

head in the clouds. __ You made a fool out of you; __ and, boy, she's

bring - ing you down. __ She made your heart melt, but you're

cold to the core. __ Now ru - mour has it she ain't got your

love an - y - more. __

Chorus

Ru - mour has it.   Ru - mour has it.   Ru - mour has it.

19

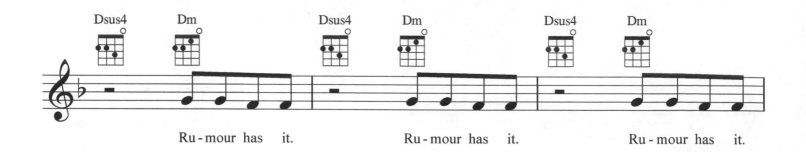

Ru-mour has it.   Ru-mour has it.   Ru-mour has it.

To Coda ⊕

Ru-mour has it.   Ru-mour has it. (Ru - mour.) —

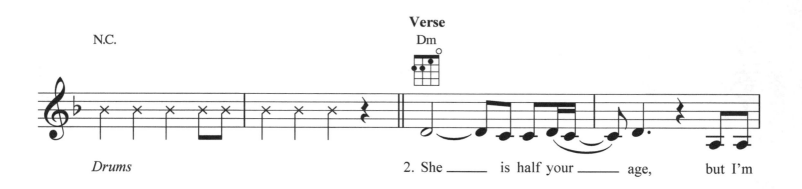

Drums   2. She _____ is half your _____ age,   but I'm

guess-ing that's the rea-son that you _____ strayed. _____   I _____ heard _____

_____ you've been miss-ing me; _____   you've been

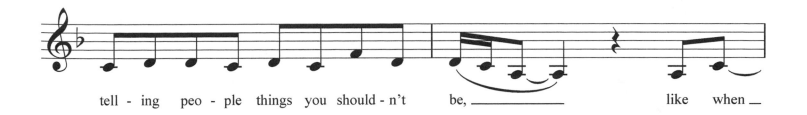

tell - ing peo - ple things you should - n't be, _____ like when _

___ we creep out when she ___ ain't a - round. Have - n't you heard the

Pre-Chorus

N.C.   Dm

ru - mours? Yes, bless your soul, you've got your head in the clouds. _ You've made a

Gm7   Bb

fool out of me; ___ and, boy, you're bring-ing me down. ___ You made my heart melt, yet I'm

Dm   Gm7   *D.S. al Coda*

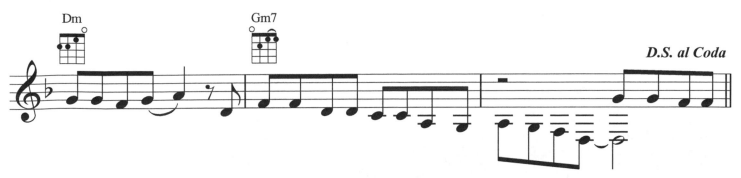

cold to the core. _ But ru - mour has it I'm the one you're leav-ing her for.
Ru - mour has it.

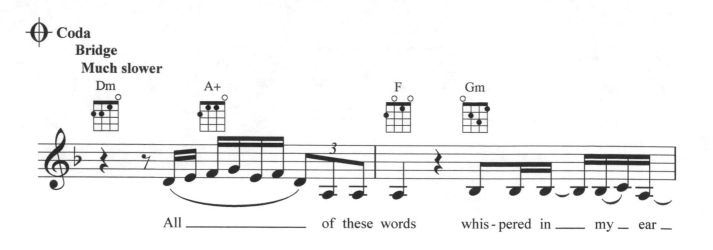

All _____ of these words whis-pered in _ my _ ear _

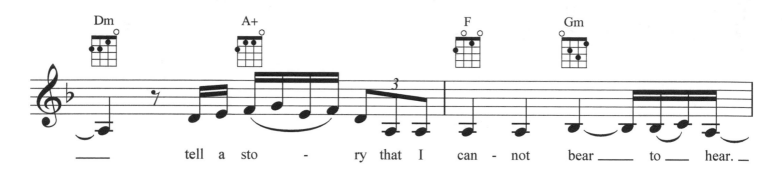

_ tell a sto - ry that I can-not bear _ to _ hear. _

_ Just 'cause I said it, it don't mean _____ that I

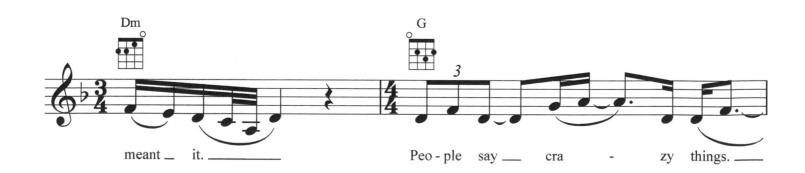

meant _ it. _____ Peo-ple say _ cra - zy things. _

_ Just 'cause I said it don't mean that I meant it, _____ just 'cause you heard it. _

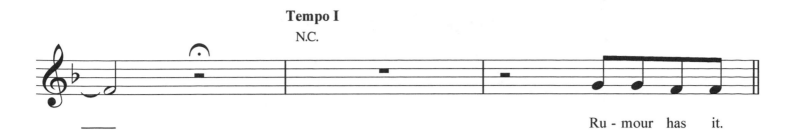

Tempo I

N.C.

Ru - mour has it.

Outro-Chorus

Dsus4 Dm Dsus4 Dm Dsus4 Dm

Ru - mour has it. Ru - mour has it. Ru - mour has it.

Dsus4 Dm Dsus4 Dm 1. Dsus4 Dm

Ru - mour has it. Ru - mour has it. Ru - mour has it.

2.

Dsus4 Dm Dsus4 Dm Dsus4 Dm

Ru - mour has it. (Ru - mour.) _ Ru - mour has it.
But

Gm N.C. Dm7

ru - mour has it he's the one I'm leav- ing you for.

Send My Love
(To Your New Lover)

Words and Music by Adele Adkins, Max Martin and Shellback

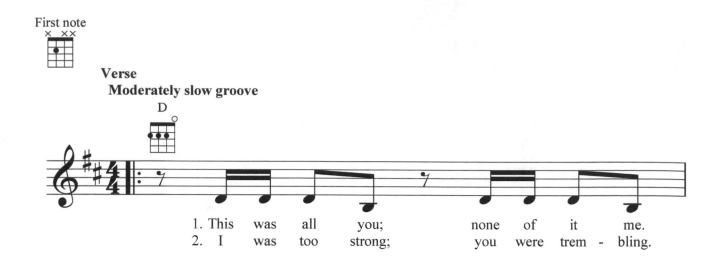

1. This was all you; none of it me.
2. I was too strong; you were trem - bling.

You put your hands on, _____ on my bod - y and
You could - n't han - dle _____ the hot heat

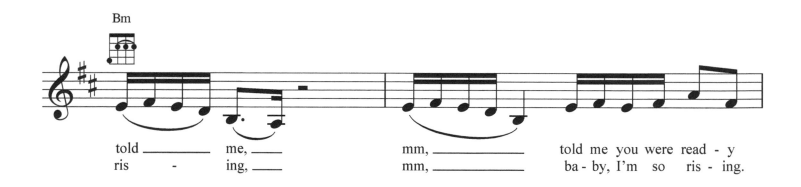

told _____ me, ____ mm, _____ told me you were read - y
ris - ing, ____ mm, _____ ba - by, I'm so ris - ing.

for the big one, for the big jump. I'd be your last love, ____ ev - er - last - ing,
I was run - ning, you were walk - ing. You could - n't keep up ____ you were fall - ing

you ____ and me. ____   Mm, _____   that was what you told   me.
down. _____   Mm, _____   there's on - ly   one ____ way down.

Pre-Chorus

I'm   giv - ing you ____ up, ____ I've   for - giv - en it _____ all. _

_____   You   set   me ____   free. _____

𝄋 Chorus

Send my love to your new lo - ov - er, _____   treat her bet - ter. __ We've

got - ta let   go   of all of our   ghosts; _   we both know we ain't kids no   more. _

Send my love to your new lo - ov - er, _____   treat her bet - ter. __ We've

got-ta let go of all of our ghosts; ___ we both know we ain't kids no more. ___

1.

2. **Bridge**

If you're read-y, ___ if you're read-y, ___ if you're read-y, ___ I'm read-y. ___

If you're read-y, ___ if you're read-y, ___ we both know we ain't kids no more. ___

___ No, _____ we ain't kids no

more. _____

Pre-Chorus

I'm giv-ing you ____ up, ____ I've for-giv-en it ____ all. ____

____ You set me ____ free. ____

Outro-Chorus

Coda

____ Send my love to your new lo - ov - er, ____

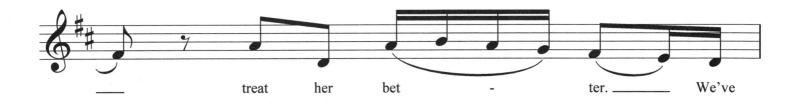

____ treat her bet - ter. ____ We've

got - ta let go of all of our ghosts; ____

we both know we ain't kids no more. ____

Set Fire to the Rain

Words and Music by Adele Adkins and Fraser Smith

First note

Verse
Pop Rock

1. I let it fall, my heart, and as it

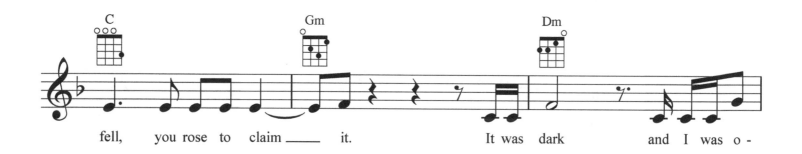

fell, you rose to claim ____ it. It was dark and I was o-

ver ____ un - til you kissed my lips ____ and you saved ____ me. 2. My

Verse

hands, they were strong, ___ but my knees were far too weak ____
(3.) lay with ___ you, ___ I could stay ____ there, ___ close ___

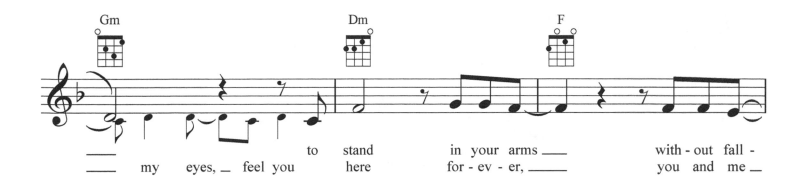

_____ my eyes, _ feel you here for - ev - er, _____ you and me _
_____ to stand in your arms _____ with - out fall -

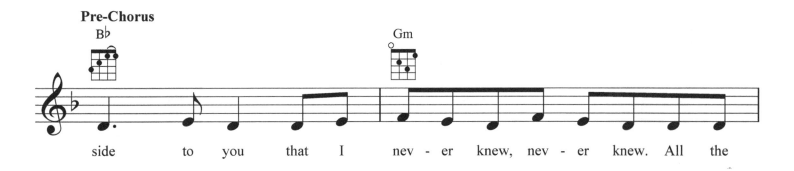

_____ to - geth - er. Noth - ing gets bet - ter. 'Cause there's a
- ing to your feet. _____ But

Pre-Chorus

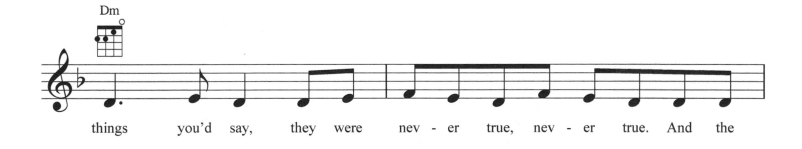

side to you that I nev - er knew, nev - er knew. All the

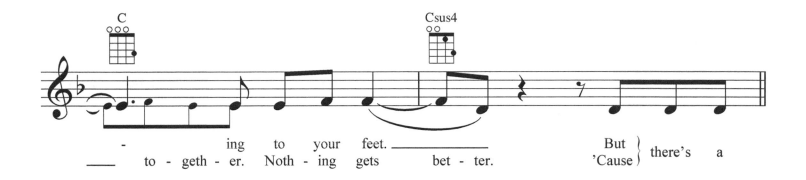

things you'd say, they were nev - er true, nev - er true. And the

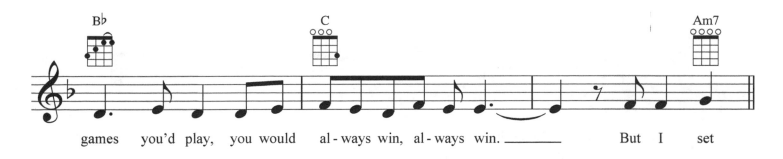

games you'd play, you would al - ways win, al - ways win. _____ But I set

fi - re _____ to the rain, watched it pour __

____ as I ____ touched your face. _____ When it burned, __

____ well, I cried ___ 'cause I heard ____ it scream - ing out your

1.

2., 3.

name, your name. _____ 3. When I _____ I set

Chorus

fi - re _____ to the rain and I threw us _____ in - to the flames. __

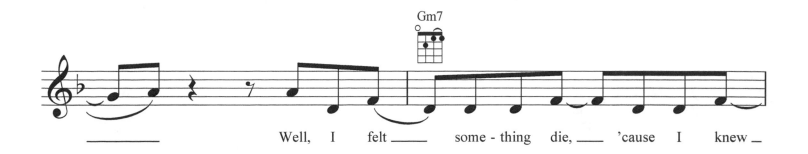

Well, I felt _____ some - thing die, _____ 'cause I knew ___

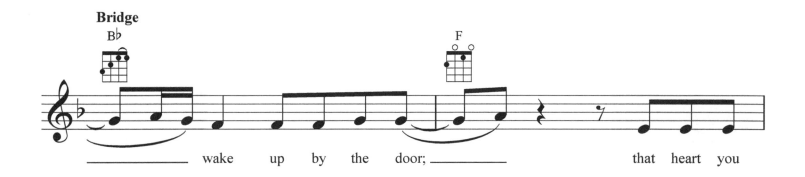

To Coda ⊕

_____ that that ___ was the last time, the last time. _____ Some - times I ___

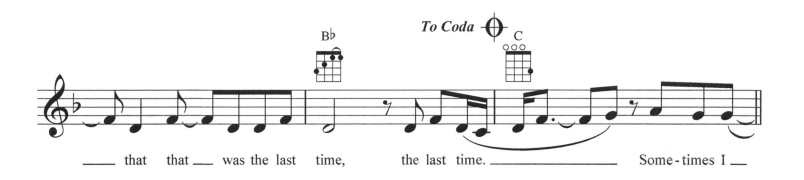

Bridge

_____ wake up by the door; _____ that heart you

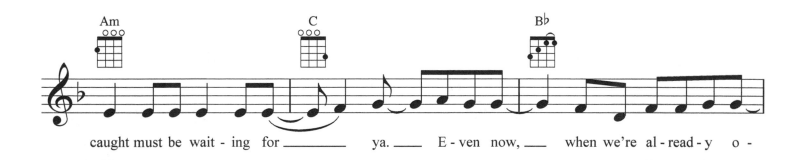

caught must be wait - ing for _____ ya. ___ E - ven now, ___ when we're al - read - y o -

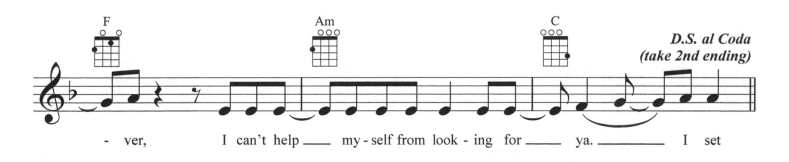

D.S. al Coda
(take 2nd ending)

- ver, I can't help ___ my - self from look - ing for _____ ya. _____ I set

Oh. Oh, no,

oh. Let it burn.

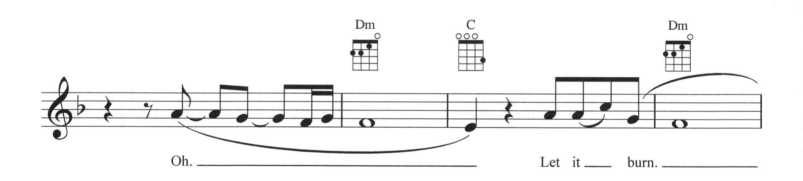

Oh. Let it burn.

Let it burn.

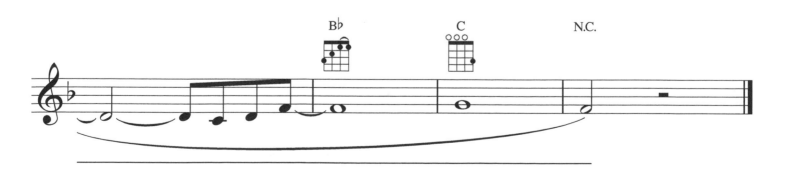

Rolling in the Deep

Words and Music by Adele Adkins and Paul Epworth

your ___ love re-mind me of ___ us. They keep me think-ing that we al-most had it

all. The scars of your ___ love, they leave me breath - less. I can't help

Chorus

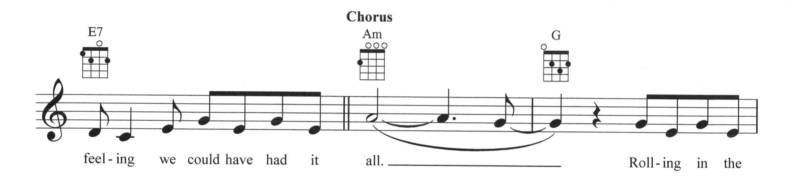

feel-ing we could have had it all. _____ Roll-ing in the

deep. _____ You had my heart in - side _____ of your hand, __

1.   *D.C.*
                                                              (take 2nd ending)

___ and you played ___ it to the beat. _____

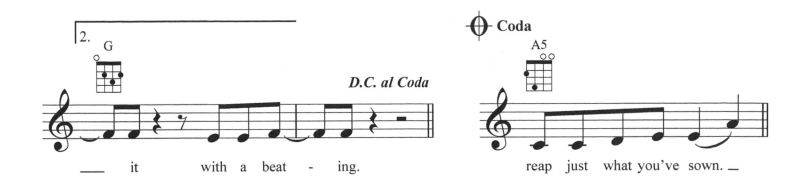

2.

D.C. al Coda

_____ it with a beat - ing.

⊕ **Coda**

reap just what you've sown. ___

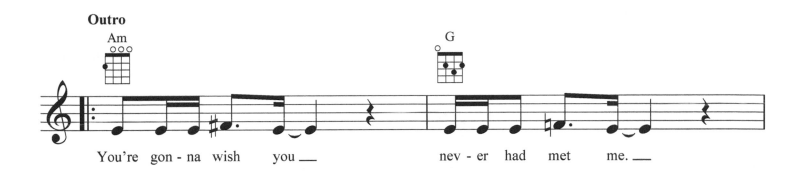

Outro

You're gon - na wish you ___ nev - er had met me. ___

Tears are gon - na fall, ___ roll - ing in the deep. ___

Additional Lyrics

2. See how I'll leave with every piece of you.
Don't underestimate the things that I will do.
There's a fire starting in my heart,
Reaching a fever pitch and it's bringing me out the dark.

3. Baby, I have no story to be told,
But I've heard one on you; now I'm gonna make your head burn.
Think of me in the depths of your despair;
Make a home down there, as mine sure won't be shared.

4. Throw your soul through every open door.
Count your blessings to find what you look for.
Turn my sorrows into treasured gold.
You'll pay me back in kind and reap just what you've sown.

Skyfall

from the Motion Picture SKYFALL
Words and Music by Adele Adkins and Paul Epworth

Swept a-way, ___ I'm stol - en. _____ Let the

𝄋 Chorus

sky fall. ___ When it crum - bles, ___ we will stand tall, _____ face it all ___

___ to - geth - er. Let the sky fall. ___ When it crum - bles, ___ we will

To Coda 🜛

stand tall, _____ face it all ___ to - geth - er at sky -

fall.   At sky - fall.

Verse

2. Sky - fall is where ___ we start, _____ a thou - sand miles ___ and

poles a - part, ___ where worlds col - lide ___ and

days are dark. _____ You may have my num - ber. ___ You can take my name, ___

but you'll nev - er have ___ my heart. _____ Let the

D.S. al Coda

Coda
Interlude

fall. Let the sky fall. When it crum - bles,

we will stand tall. Let the sky fall.

When it crum - bles, we will stand tall.

Water Under the Bridge

Words and Music by Adele Adkins and Gregory Kurstin

Someone Like You

Words and Music by Adele Adkins and Dan Wilson

1. I _____ heard that you're set-tled down, _ that you

found a girl _ and you're mar-ried now. _____

_____ I heard _ that your dreams came true. Guess she

gave you things _____ I did-n't give to you. _____

Old friend, why are you so _____ shy? _____ Ain't like you to hold __ back __ or __ hide _____ from the light. __ I

Pre-Chorus

hate to turn up _____ out of the blue un - in - vit - ed, but I _____ _____ could - n't stay a - way, _____ I could - n't fight it. I had hoped you'd see my face and that you'd be re - mind - ed that, for me, _____ it is - n't o - ver. _____

time — flies, — on - ly — yes - ter - day — was the

time of our lives. — We — were born and — raised — in a

sum - mer haze, — bound by the — sur - prise of our

Pre-Chorus

glo - ry — days. — I hate to turn up — out of the blue un - in - vit- ed, but I —

— could - n't stay a - way, — I could - n't fight it. I had

hoped you'd see my face and that you'd be re - mind - ed that, for

D.S. al Coda

me, _____ it is - n't o - ver. _____

Coda

lasts in love, but some - times it hurts in -

Bridge

- stead." _____ Noth - ing com - pares, no wor - ries or cares, re -

grets and mis - takes, they're mem - o - ries made.

Who would have known how _____ bit - ter - sweet _____ this would

Chorus

taste? Nev - er mind, _ I'll _ find _ some - one like _____

you. I wish noth-ing but the best for you.

Don't for - get me, I beg. I re -

mem - ber you said, "Some - times it

lasts in love, but some - times it hurts in -

1. - stead." 2. - stead." Some-times it

Outro

lasts in love, but some-times it hurts in - stead.

When We Were Young

Words and Music by Adele Adkins and Tobias Jesso Jr.

First note

Verse
Moderately

Dm   F
1. Ev - 'ry - bod - y loves the things you do, ___

Bb   F   Gm7
___ from the way you talk ___ to the way you move. ___

F   Dm   F
___ Ev - 'ry - bod - y here is watch -

Bb   F   Gm7
- ing you, ___ 'cause you feel like ___ home, ___ you're like a dream come ___

Verse
F   Dm   F
___ true.
2. But if by chance you're here a -
3. I was so scared to face my

53

it is the last time that we might be ex-act-ly like we were

be-fore we re-al-ized we were sad of get-ting old. It made us rest-

less. It was just like a mov-ie, it was just like a

song. song (when we

were young, when we were young, when we

were young, when we were young.) It's hard